W9-AGZ-116

SCOTT FORESMAN
READING STREET

Animals, Tame and Wild

Program Authors

Connie Juel, Ph.D.

Jeanne R. Paratore, Ed.D.

Deborah Simmons, Ph.D.

Sharon Vaughn, Ph.D.

ISBN: 0-328-21426-4
Copyright © 2008 Pearson Education, Inc.

All Rights Reserved. Printed in the United States of America. This publication is protected by Copyright, and permission should be obtained from the publisher prior to any prohibited reproduction, storage in a retrieval system, or transmission in any form by any means, electronic, mechanical, photocopying, recording, or otherwise. For information regarding permission(s), write to: Permissions Department, Scott Foresman, 1900 East Lake Avenue, Glenview, Illinois 60025.

10 V003 12 11 10 09

CC1

PEARSON
Scott Foresman

Editorial Offices: Glenview, Illinois • Parsippany, New Jersey • New York, New York
Sales Offices: Boston, Massachusetts • Duluth, Georgia • Glenview, Illinois
Coppell, Texas • Sacramento, California • Mesa, Arizona

UNIT 1 Contents

Animals, Tame and Wild

Animal Friends

Taking Care of Pets 4
How do people take care of pets?

People Help Animals 20
How can people help animals?

Animals Help People 40
How can animals help people?

MY SIDEWALKS ON
SCOTT FORESMAN
READING STREET

Wild Animals

See the Animals 60

How can we learn about animals by watching them?

Animal Neighbors 86

Which wild animals can we find in our neighborhood?

Animals Around the World 118

How can we help animals around the world?

Contents

Taking Care of Pets

Let's Find Out

6 **Taking Care of Pets**
Show your pet that you care.

10 **What Pets Like**
See what makes pets happy.

14 **Pets on a Mat**
Who will fit on the mat?

18 **Which Is a Pet?**
Is it wild? Is it a pet?

See page 19 for My New Words and Pictionary!

Let's Find Out

Taking Care of PETS

I like the bird.

I like the cat.

I like the fish.

I like the dog.

What Pets Like

by Annie Nelson
illustrated by Wayne Parmenter

The fish like the tank.

The kittens like the mouse.

The birds like the toy.

The puppies like the towel.

Pets on a Mat

by Julian Cove • illustrated by Chris Lensch

I like the mat.

I like the mat.

I like the mat.

I like the mat.

WHICH IS A PET?

Read Together

cat

turtle

moose

fish

turkey

dog

tiger

monkey

My New Words

I*	**I** am in first grade.
like*	I **like** puppies.
the*	What is **the** name of your pet?

*tested high-frequency words

Pictionary

kitten

puppy

Sam
can sit!

People Help Animals

Let's Find Out

22 **People Help Animals**
Who helps animals? Find out.

26 **Pam and Tam Tam**
A puppy goes to the vet.

32 **Sit, Sam!**
Can Tim teach his puppy to sit?

38 **Old MacDonald Had a Farm**
Sing a song about animals.

See page 39 for My New Words and Pictionary!

Let's Find Out

People Help Animals

I am a vet.

I am a firefighter.

I am a dog walker.

I am a zookeeper.

Pam and Tam Tam

by Madison Wetzel
illustrated by Carolyn Croll

Pam is a vet.

Tam Tam is a puppy.

I look at Tam Tam.

I pat Tam Tam.

Tam Tam sat.

I like Tam Tam.

Sit, Sam!

by Percy Scott • illustrated by Ana Ochoa

I am Tim.

Sam is a puppy.

Sit, Sam, sit.

Look at Sam sit.

I pat Sam.

Pat, pat, pat.

Sam pats Tim!

Old MacDonald Had a Farm

Sing Together

Old MacDonald had a farm, E–I–E–I–O.
And on his farm he had a dog, E–I–E–I–O.
With a "woof, woof" here,
And a "woof, woof" there,
Here a "woof," there a "woof,"
Everywhere a "woof, woof."
Old MacDonald had a farm, E–I–E–I–O!

woof

2nd verse: cat meow

3rd verse: cow moo

4th verse: pig oink

My New Words

a*	Here is **a** pen.
is*	**Is** he coming to your party? It **is** hot outside.
look*	**Look** at the puppy.

*tested high-frequency words

Pictionary

firefighter

vet

Contents

Animals Help People

Let's Find Out

42 **Animals Help People**
See how animals help.

46 **What We Like**
We like what animals give us.

54 **Bob and Tom**
Ride with Bob and Tom!

58 **Did You Know?**
Some dogs have important jobs.

See page 59 for My New Words and Pictionary!

Let's Find Out

Animals Help People

Look at the camel.

Look at the cow.

Look at the sheep.

Look at the dog.

What We Like

by Grace Chin • illustrated by Christine Schneider

You have a chicken.

We like the eggs.

You have bees.

We like the honey.

You have a cow.

We like the milk.

You have a horse.

We like you.

BOB and TOM
by Jeb Wilson
illustrated by Guy Francis
I am Bob.
I am Tom.

We have a cab.

We like the cab.

We like you, Bob!
We like you, Tom!

Read Together

Did You Know?

Dogs have good noses. They can smell much better than people. Dogs can sniff things out.

Dogs can find people who are lost.

Dogs can save people trapped in snow.

My New Words

have* I **have** a nickel in my pocket.

we* **We** are in the same class.

you* **You** can use my bike.

*tested high-frequency words

Pictionary

camel

honey

Contents

See the Animals

Let's Find Out

62 **See the Animals**
What will you see?

70 **Little Cat**
See what Little Cat can do.

78 **The Ram Race**
Which ram will win?

84 **What's for Dinner?**
What do animals like to eat?

See page 85 for My New Words and Pictionary!

Look at the seals.

Can you see the little seal?
Can you see its mom?

Look on top.

Monkeys are on top.

Look at the bears.

Can you see the little bear?
It naps.

See the little cat.

Its mom can not nap!

See Little Cat.

See its mom and dad.

Little Cat is tan.

Its mom and dad are tan.

Little Cat taps on its dad.

Its mom and dad sit.

Little Cat can nap.

Its mom and dad can nap.

The Ram Race

by Lin Tam • illustrated by Andy Elkerton

See little Dan Rat.
See little Nan Rat.

Dan and Nan are on Bob Ram.

Bob ran and ran.
Dan did not sit on Bob!

Nan did not sit on Bob.
Dan and Nan did not look!

Bob ran and ran.
Dan and Nan did look!

Dan and Nan pat Bob Ram.

What's for Dinner?

Read Together

This is a lion.
What does it eat?

This is a giraffe.
What does it eat?

This is a buffalo.
What does it eat?

This is a shark.
What does it eat?

Answers: Lions eat meat. Giraffes eat leaves and branches.
Buffalo eat grass. Sharks eat other fish.

My New Words

are* Sam and Bob **are** ready.

little* A bee is **little**.

see* If you look in the box, you will **see** a toy.

*tested high-frequency words

Pictionary

nap

seal

Contents

Animal Neighbors

Let's Find Out

88 **Animal Neighbors**
What plays in your backyard?

96 **What Do They See?**
Animals live in different places.

104 **Kep**
What does Kep see?

116 **Who Is Hiding?**
Can you spot the animals?

See page 117 for My New Words and Pictionary!

Let's Find Out
Animal Neighbors
Kass can see rabbits nap.

They nap in the tin pot.

Kip can see tan birds sip.

He can see tan birds go.

Kass and Kip can see a cob.

Squirrels nip at it.

Kass and Kip sit.

Kass and Kip can look.
Can you?

What Do They See?

by Alex Karpik • illustrated by Erika Le Barre

Biff can look at mountains.

Biff can see fat bears.

Don and Kim can go and look.

They can see fins.

Kit sits on sand.

He can see a tan cat nap.

Cam can sit in a tree.

Cam can see deer.

Kep
by Rafael Cortez
illustrated by Jenny Harris
Kep is a fat, tan cat.

Kep can sit.
Kep can look.

Kep can see squirrels.

He can see red birds.

Kep ran at the red birds.
He can not go like birds.

Kep ran at the squirrels.
They ran and ran.

Can Kep nab birds?
Kep can not.

Can Kep nab squirrels?
Kep can not.

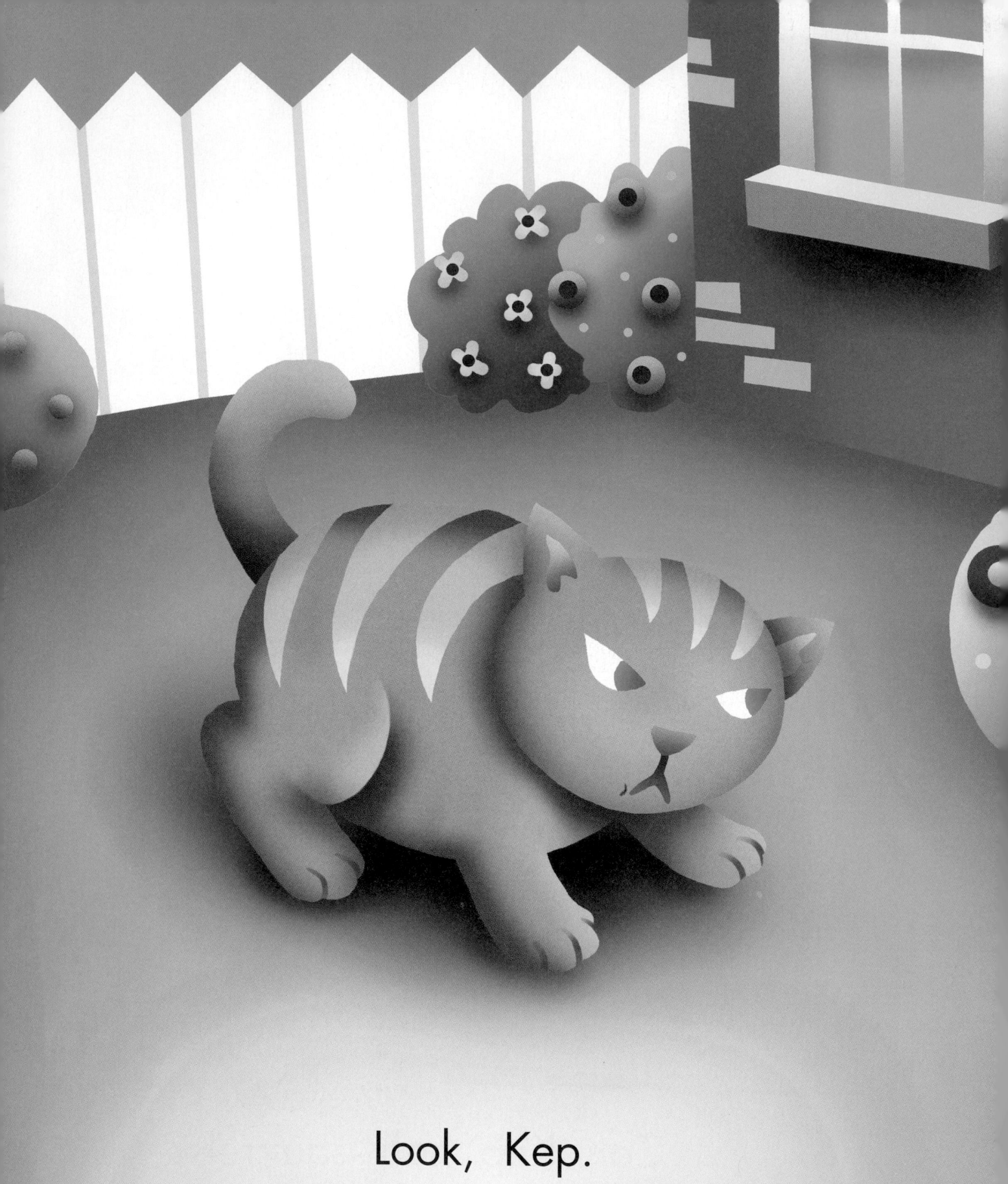

Look, Kep.

It is a mat.

Kep did not nab red birds.

Kep did not nab squirrels.

Kep did nab a nap.

Read Together

Who Is Hiding?

Read each clue.
Find the hidden animals in the picture.

1. I eat nuts and have a bushy tail.
2. I have feathers.
3. I am green and croak.
4. I hop and like carrots.

My New Words

go*	Are you ready to **go**?
he*	**He** is my friend.
nab	If you **nab** something, you grab and get it.
they*	**They** are both my friends.

*tested high-frequency words

Pictionary

mountains

fin

Contents

Animals Around the World

Let's Find Out

120 **Animals Around the World**
What animals can you see?

128 **At the Zoo**
Animals need care.

134 **Nell Can Help**
A whale needs help.

142 **Riddle Time**
Guess who I am!

See page 143 for My New Words and Pictionary!

Let's Find Out
Animals Around the World
Ann hid in the hot sand.

She can see rabbits hop.
Hip, hop, hip, hop.

Ann can see ten animals.

Can you see ten?

Hap, Rob, and Dad hid.

They can see frogs.

Do frogs hop on top of pads?
Hip, hop, hip, hop!

Dad, Hap, and Rob see ten animals.

Can you see ten?

At the Zoo

by Hunter Lobell

illustrated by Karen Lee Schmidt

Bill fed Hal.

Hal is a hippo.

Lin can mop an elephant.
She can mop at the tip top of it.

Del let a zebra run in the pen.
It ran and ran and ran.

Bill, Lin, and Del do a lot.

Animals like Bill, Lin, and Del.

Nell Can Help

by Nikolas Alexander illustrated by Liz Allen

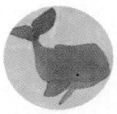

A sad whale is in mud and sand.

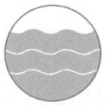

It can not go back in the water.

Nell can run.
She can run and tell.

Lots of men huff and puff.
They huff and puff in the hot sun.

Can Nell huff and puff?

Nell can huff and puff.

The men and Nell can do it!

The whale is not in mud and sand.

The whale is back in the water.

Read Together

Riddle Time

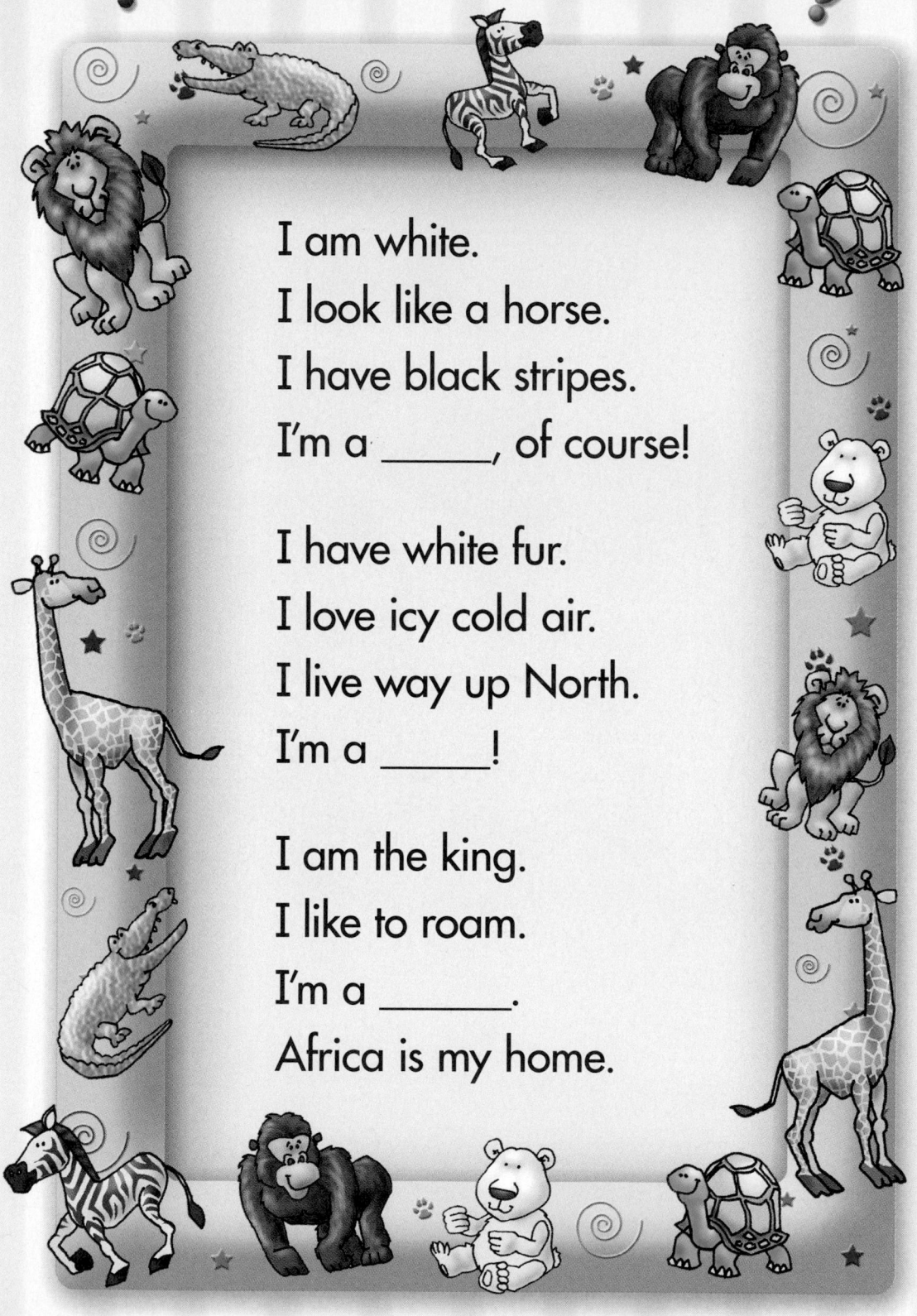

I am white.
I look like a horse.
I have black stripes.
I'm a _____, of course!

I have white fur.
I love icy cold air.
I live way up North.
I'm a _____!

I am the king.
I like to roam.
I'm a _____.
Africa is my home.

Answers: zebra, polar bear, lion

My New Words

do* Did you **do** your homework?

of* Here is a box **of** books.

she* My mother said **she** would drive.

***tested high-frequency words**

Pictionary

animals

pad

Acknowledgments

Illustrations

Opener: Andy Elkerton, Christine Schneider, Maggie Swanson, Chris Lensch; **2, 10–13** Wayne Parmenter; **3, 86, 104, 106–112, 114** Jenny B. Harris; **4, 14–17** Chris Lensch; **5, 18** Maggie Swanson; **20, 32–37** Ana Ochoa; **21, 26–31** Carolyn Croll; **21, 38** Rose Mary Berlin; **40–41, 54–57** Guy Francis; **46–53, 59** Christine Schneider; **60, 78–83** Andy Elkerton; **61, 84** Steve Cox; **87, 96–103** Erika Le Barre; **87, 116, 118, 134–136, 138, 140–141** Elizabeth Allen; **88, 90–94, 142** Jason Wolff; **119, 128–133** Karen Lee Schmidt; **120–122, 124–126** Kellie Lewis; **142** Don Tate

Photographs

Every effort has been made to secure permission and provide appropriate credit for photographic material. The publisher deeply regrets any omission and pledges to correct errors called to its attention in subsequent editions.

Unless otherwise acknowledged, all photographs are the property of Scott Foresman, a division of Pearson Education.

Photo locators denoted as follows: Top (T), Center (C), Bottom (B), Left (L), Right (R), Background (Bkgd).

Opener: ©Aura/Getty Images; **2** (TR, BL) Getty Images; **3** Getty Images; **5** Getty Images; **6** (C, BR, TL, TC) Getty Images, (TR) ©Renee Lynn/Getty Images, (TC) Steve Shott/©DK Images; **7** (C) ©Aura/Getty Images, (BC) Getty Images; **8** (C) Comstock Images, (BC) Max Gibbs/©DK Images; **9** (C) ©Ariel Skelley/Corbis, (BR) Getty Images; **19** (BR, C) Getty Images; **22** (C) ©Ron Levine/Getty Images, (BC) ©Christopher Bissell/Getty Images; **23** (C) ©Jochen Tack/Alamy Images, (BC) ©Rubberball Productions/Getty Images; **24** ©Kate Powers/Getty Images; **25** (C) ©Paddy Ryan/Animals Animals/Earth Scenes, (BC) ©Royalty-Free/Corbis; **39** (BR) ©Rubberball Productions/Getty Images, (BC) ©Christopher Bissell/Getty Images; **41** Getty Images; **42** (C) ©Dallas and John Heaton/Stock Connection, (BC) ©GK & Vikki Hart/Getty Images; **43** (C) Ron Redfern/©DK Images, (BC) ©Catherine Ledner/Getty Images; **44** (C) ©Nigel Cattlin/Photo Researchers, Inc., (BC) Getty Images, (BR) ©Alice Edward/Getty Images; **45** (BC) Getty Images, (C) ©Photofusion Picture Library/Alamy Images; **58** ©Mauro Fermariello/Photo Researchers, Inc.; **59** ©GK & Vikki Hart/Getty Images; **61** ©Daryl Balfour/Getty Images; **62** (C, BC) Jupiter Images; **63** Jupiter Images; **64** ©Theo Allofs/Getty Images; **65** ©Theo Allofs/Getty Images; **66** (C, BC) Getty Images; **67** Getty Images; **68** ©Anup Shah/Nature Picture Library; **70** ©Mike Hill/Alamy Images; **72** (C) ©Daryl Balfour/Getty Images, (CL) ©Mitsuaki Iwago/Minden Pictures; **73** ©Angela Scott/Getty Images; **74** ©Art Wolfe/Getty Images; **75** ©Mitch Reardon/Getty Images; **76** ©Juniors Bildarchiv/Alamy Images; **77** ©Image Source/Getty Images; **85** Getty Images; **117** (C, BC) Getty Images; **143** (CL, C, CR, BL) Getty Images